MW00912055

Where Do Fossils Come from?

How Do We Find Them?
Archaeology for Kids

Children's Biological Science of Fossils Books

BOBO'S
LITTLE BRIANIAC BOOKS

educational & informative books for children
(PRE-K / K-12)

Copyright 2016

All Rights reserved. No part of this book may be reproduced or used in any way or form or by any means whether electronic or mechanical, this means that you cannot record or photocopy any material ideas or tips that are provided in this book

What was life like millions of years ago? Have you ever tried to imagine it? How did we know that dinosaurs existed? How did we know what they look like? How did we know that dinosaurs with feathers existed? How do we find records of a world that disappeared long ago?

We can trace life forms over millions of years by studying fossils.

Palaeontology is a branch of biology that studies ancient humans, plants and animals who lived in prehistoric times by studying fossils. People who study fossils are called palaeontologists.

By this study, we know what dinosaurs looked like, how the first humans looked, and where they lived. This is science. It really amazes us with its discoveries.

Palaeontologists often dig little holes and huge sites to get fossils. But sometimes fossils just show up through the actions of man or nature.

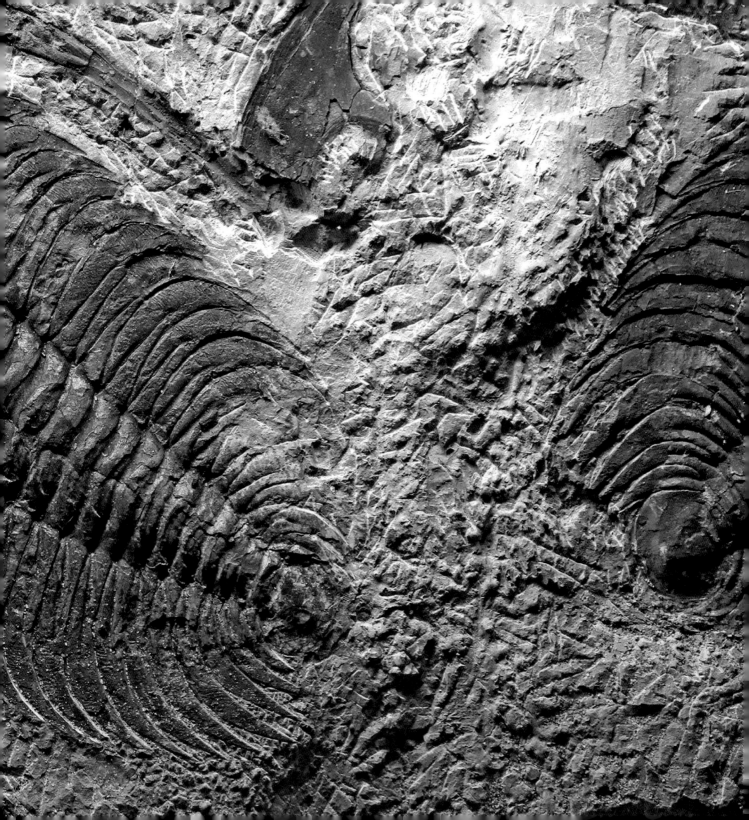

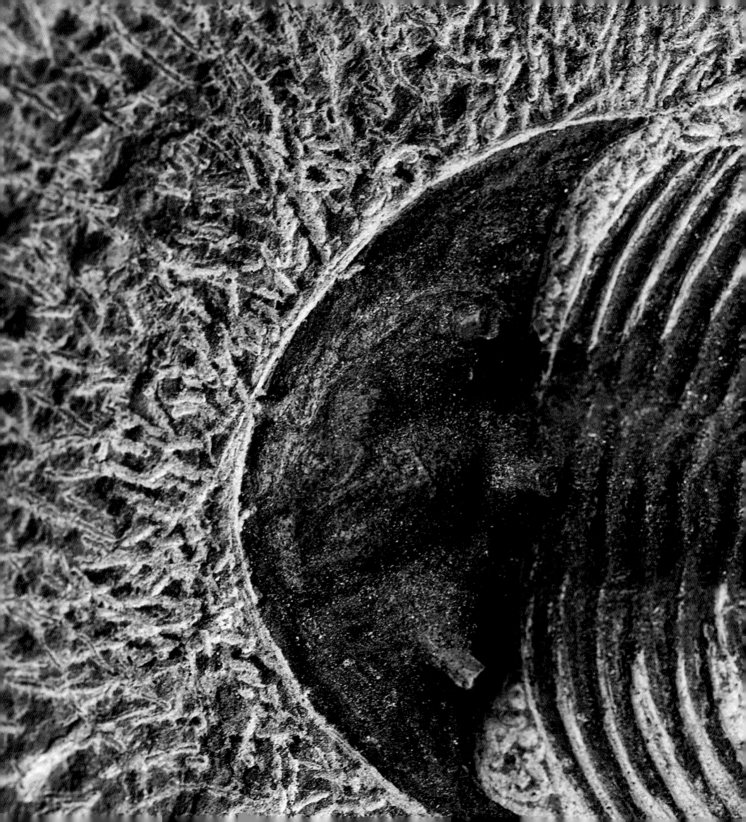

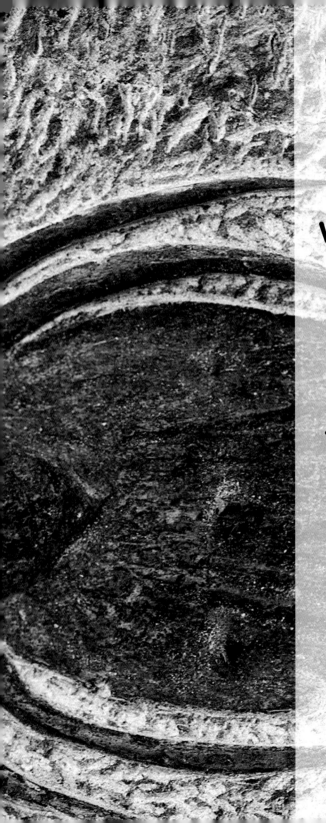

What are fossils? "Fossil" comes from the Latin word fossilis. This means "to dig up". Fossils are the remains of forms of life from past geologic ages that have been squeezed and buried in sedimentary rocks.

Fossils tell us the activities, origins, and physical attributes of ancient forms of life. Fossils can be found anywhere in all continents.

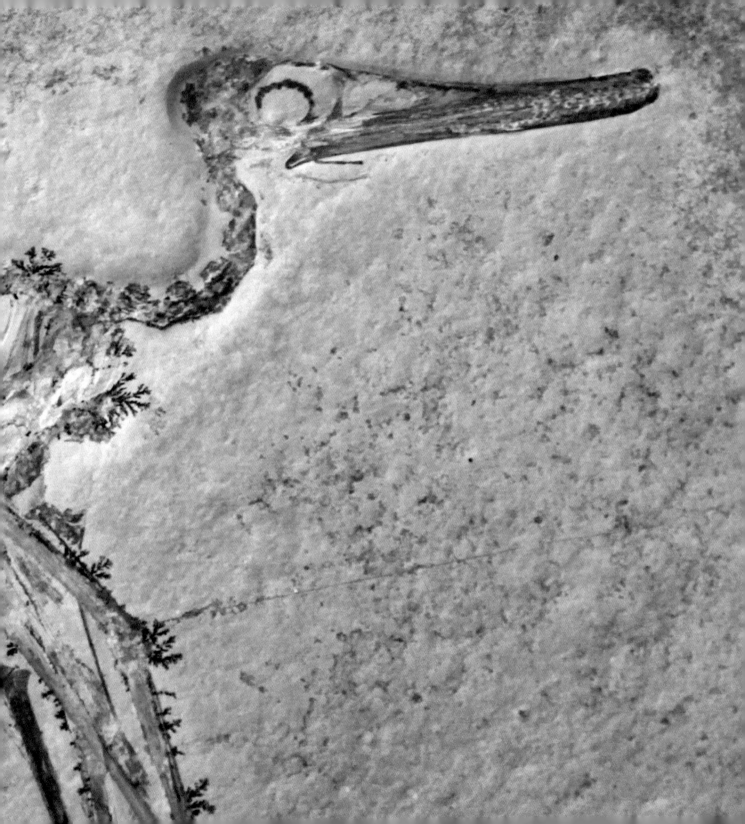

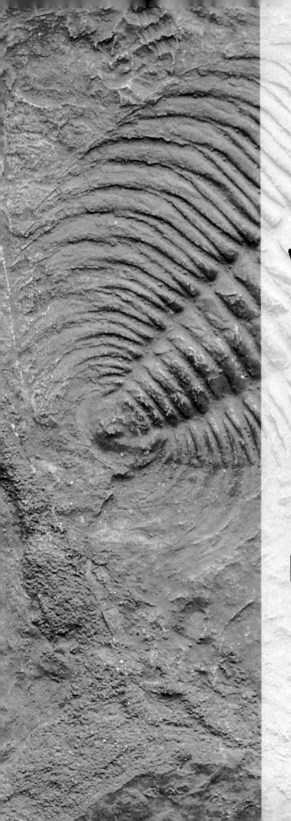

They are usually found in sedimentary rocks which were formed from small pieces of rocks, mud and sand. For years, the sand and small rocks built up and hardened in layers, with the fossils included in some of the layers.

What do fossils or their traces look like? Did they retain their original form? Are they always like a fossilized bone? No. A fossilized bone doesn't contain any bone any more though it has the shape of a bone. It is more of a rock.

How are fossils formed? Ancient forms of life like animals got buried immediately after their death. They sank into the mud or were buried in sandstorms.

Their remains would become part of the sediment. Over millions of years, more sediment would cover these remains making it more part of the rock than its original form.

What parts were usually fossilized? The bones and teeth of animals, or hard body parts, sink into the sediment and stay there for millions of years, waiting to be excavated.

Over time, these remains would take on the appearance of rocks through a series of chemical changes. Water with minerals would sink into the objects, giving them a rock-like appearance. In this process the minerals in the decaying object were dissolved and replaced with minerals from the sediment.

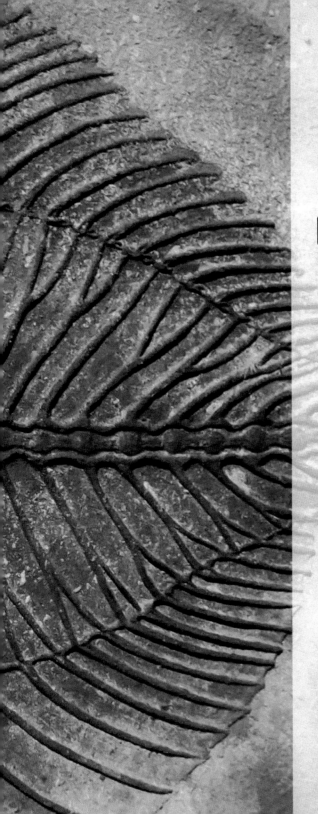

This is called permineralization: filling fossils with minerals. This also involved the process of recrystallization in which minerals changed their form.

Another way of forming fossils was by petrification. In this process, the hard and soft parts of the decaying object are replaced with other minerals such as calcite and silica. In this process, the remains were not turned to stones.

Some remains, like those of insects, became pressed into tree resin which turned to amber over the years. But not all ancient forms of life were fossilized. They simply died, decayed and were lost.

The end products of this fossilization process were heavy rock-like objects.

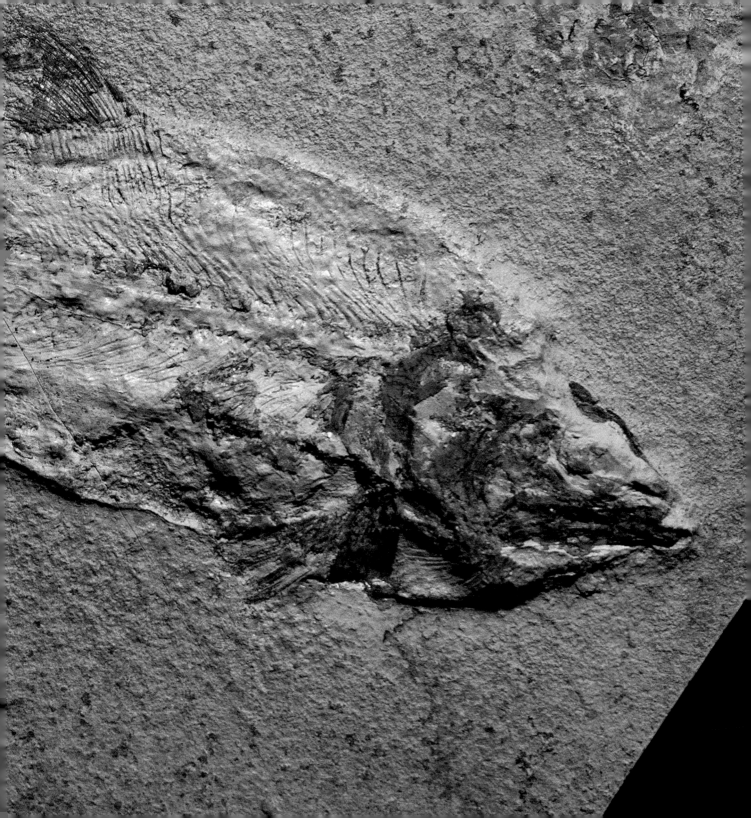

But not all fossils were bones and teeth of animals. Fossils also include animal footprints and their burrows. Usually, scientists would not find the whole animal. Instead, they just excavated shells, teeth and bones.

Aren't these facts about fossils amazing? Yes, definitely. Fossils are amazing. With their help, we can imagine how life was when the world was much, much younger. Kids, it's an adventure to trace back to see how things were millions of years ago.

Made in the USA
Monee, IL
18 August 2022

11948479R00026